TABLE OF CONTENTS

ENGLISH SHORT STORIES

FOR BEGINNERS AND

INTERMEDIATE LEARNERS

Engaging Short Stories to Learn
English and Build Your Vocabulary

2nd Edition

LANGUAGE GURU

ISBN: 978-1-950321-28-5

INTRODUCTION

We all know that immersion is the tried and true way to learn a foreign language. After all, it's how we got so good at our first language. The problem is that it's extremely difficult to recreate the same circumstances when we learn a foreign language. We come to rely so much on our native language for everything, and it's hard to make enough time to learn a new one.

We aren't surrounded by the foreign language in our home countries. More often than not, our families can't speak this new language we want to learn. And many of us have stressful jobs or demanding classes that eat away at our limited energy and hours of the day. Immersion can seem like an impossibility.

What we can do, however, is gradually work our way up to immersion no matter where we are in life. And the way we can do this is through extensive reading and listening.

If you have ever taken a foreign language class, chances are you are familiar with intensive reading and listening. In intensive reading and listening, a small amount of text or a short audio recording is broken down line by line, and then, you are drilled on grammar endlessly.

Extensive reading and listening, on the other hand, is quite the opposite. You read a large number of pages or listen to hours and hours of the foreign language without worrying about understanding everything. You rely on context for meaning and try to limit the number of words you need to look up.

If you ask the most successful language learners, it's not intensive but extensive reading and listening that delivers the best results. Simply, volume is much more effective than explicit explanations and rote memorization.

To be able to read like this comfortably, you must practice reading in the foreign language for hours every single day. It takes a massive volume of text before your brain stops intensively reading and shifts into extensive reading.

This book hopes to provide a few short stories in English you can use to practice extensive reading. These stories were written and edited by native English speakers from the United States. We hope these short stories help build confidence in your overall reading comprehension skills and encourage you to read more native material. They offer supplementary reading practice with a heavy focus on teaching vocabulary words.

Vocabulary is the number one barrier to entry to extensive reading. Without an active vocabulary base of 10,000 words or more, you'll be stuck constantly looking up words in the dictionary, which will be sure to slow down your reading early on. To speed up the rate at which you read, building and maintaining a vast vocabulary range is absolutely vital. This is why it's so important to invest as much time as possible into immersing yourself in native English every single day. This includes both reading and listening as well as being around native speakers through any and all means possible.

We hope you enjoy the book and find it useful in growing your English vocabulary and bringing you a few steps closer to extensive reading and fluency!

HOW TO USE THIS BOOK

To simulate extensive reading better, we recommend keeping things simple and using the short stories in the following manner. Read through each story just once and no more. In general, whenever you encounter a word you don't know, first try to guess its meaning using the surrounding context. If its meaning is still unclear and the word is in **bold**, check that chapter's vocabulary list for a very simplified definition. If the unknown word is not in bold, a quick online dictionary search may be required.

In our vocabulary lists, we have strived both to include as many potentially new words and phrases as possible but also to keep each list as brief as possible. As a result, we left out a great deal of words that can be understood via context as well as many basic words.

In addition, it's also recommended to read each story silently. While reading aloud can seem beneficial for pronunciation and intonation, it's a practice more aligned with intensive reading. It will further slow down your reading pace and make it considerably more difficult for you to get into extensive reading. If you want to work on pronunciation and intonation, consider practicing these during study and review times rather than reading time. Alternatively, you could also speak to a English tutor or friend to practice what you learned.

After completing the reading for each chapter, test your knowledge of the story by answering the comprehension questions.

Check your answers using the answer key located at the end of the book.

As a means of review, memorization of any kind is completely unnecessary for language acquisition. The actual language acquisition process occurs subconsciously, and any effort to memorize new vocabulary and grammar structures only stores this information in your short-term memory. Attempting to force new information into your long-term memory only serves to eat up your time and make it that much more frustrating when you can't recall it in the future.

If you wish to review new information that you have learned from the short stories, there are several options that would be wiser. Spaced Repetition Systems (SRS) allow you to cut down on your review time by setting specific intervals in which you are tested on information in order to promote long-term memory storage. Anki and the Goldlist Method are two popular SRS choices that give you the ability to review whatever information you'd like from whatever material you'd like.

Trying to actively review every single new thing you learn, however, will slow you down on your overall path to fluency. While there may be hundreds or even thousands of sentences you want to practice and review, perhaps the best way to go about internalizing it all is to forget it. If it's that important, it will come up through more reading and listening to more English. Languages are more effectively acquired when we allow ourselves to read and listen to them naturally.

And with that, it is time to get started with our main character John and the ten stories about his life. Good luck, reader!

CHAPTER ONE: ILLNESS AND MEDICINE

For the past few days, John had had some **difficulty breathing**. He was 30 years old, and it was a bit **odd** for someone of his age to have this **symptom**. Maybe if he was a **smoker**, things would **make** more **sense**, but John had never smoked a **cigarette** in his life. He decided to go see his doctor about it.

Luckily, he was able to **schedule an appointment** that very week and **get himself checked out**. At the doctor's office, there was a **considerable** waiting **period** before you could be seen by the **physician**. John brought a book to read in the waiting room, but he **found it** hard to **focus** for very long, **given** his **condition**. After 20 minutes, he started to get a **splitting headache**. **In anticipation** of such a **scenario**, he kept **over-the-counter pain relievers** in his car. **Following** a quick trip and back, he **washed down** the **pills** with water from the **water fountain** and **took** a big **sigh of relief**.

The nurse **called** John back to room 107 and did some **routine check-up procedures**. She **took** his blood **pressure, measured** his **height** and **weight**, and asked about his family's history of health problems. John was **fortunate** enough to not have any **hereditary** health **issues**. There was no heart **disease, cancer, diabetes**, nor **arthritis** to worry about. The nurse also asked about any and all **current** drugs he was taking, but he **replied** that he doesn't take any **medication**.

After John's information was recorded, the nurse left the **examination** room and told him the doctor would be with him shortly. Just two minutes later, he was finally **face to face** with the man who could help **cure** him **in no time**. Dr. Spetzel was his name, and he was as friendly as could be. The two chatted about John's breathing issue, and John **went into** more **detail** about his condition. **Chest** pains were **occurring throughout** the day, but there were no heart **palpitations**. There was a little **coughing** but no **wheezing**. The doctor **placed** his **stethoscope** on John's chest and asked him to take a couple of deep breaths.

With a few **subtle nods**, it **appeared** Dr. Spetzel had **reached** a final **diagnosis**. It was **asthma**. He said it was **common** for adults to **develop** asthma and not just children. An **inhaler** would immediately **curb** his symptoms, but it was a medication he would be **required** to take for the rest of his life to **keep** his symptoms **at bay**.

Carrying his **prescription** from Dr. Spetzel, John **headed towards** the **pharmacy** to receive his inhaler. He **dropped it off** at the **customer service desk** then started to **wander** around the store. It would be some time until his **prescription was filled**, so he **browsed** the various medicines on the store's **shelves**. He saw **tons** of **products** to **treat** colds, **allergies**, and the **flu**. There were even over-the-counter treatments for **constipation** and **diarrhea**.

The **pharmacist called out** to John, for it was time to **pick up** his prescription and head back home. While out in his car in the **parking lot**, John took his first **dose** and **instantly** felt much better. It became **significantly** easier to breathe, and his chest pains **subsided**. He was **grateful** for the **miracle** of modern science and medicine.

Throughout the **ordeal**, it occurred to John how important his health and body were to him. Being in a **constant state** of bad health would make for a very poor **quality of life**. His **diet** would be the first place to start making **improvements**.

Vocabulary

- **illness** --- when you are sick

- **difficulty (trouble)** --- a problem

- **breathing** --- taking air into and out of your lungs

- **odd** --- strange

- **symptom** --- a problem from an even bigger problem

- **smoker** --- a person who smokes tobacco regularly

- **make sense** --- to be easy to understand

- **cigarette** --- tobacco rolled in thin paper for smoking

- **luckily** --- because of good luck

- **schedule an appointment** --- to arrange a meeting with someone

- **get sth. checked out** --- to go to an expert to check sth.

- **considerable** --- large or important

- **period (time)** --- a time that starts and ends

- **physician** --- a doctor *(who is not a surgeon)*

- **find something ...** --- to think that something is ...

- **focus [verb]** --- to put work into only one thing

- **given [preposition]** --- when you think about something

- **condition (state)** --- how something is doing

- **splitting headache** --- a very bad pain in your head

- **in anticipation** --- getting ready for something to happen

- **scenario (event)** --- a possible future

- **over-the-counter** --- drugs that can be bought without a doctor

- **pain relievers** --- medicines that reduce pain

- **following [preposition]** --- after

- **wash down (drink)** --- to drink sth. after eating or taking medicine

- **pills** --- small pieces of medicine you take by swallowing

- **water fountain** --- a machine you drink water from

- **take (do)** --- used with nouns to say someone is doing something

- **sigh of relief** --- a relaxing breath you take after a difficult time

- **call (ask to come)** --- to ask somebody to come somewhere

- **routine [adjective]** --- done as a normal part of a job

- **check-up** --- a check done by an expert of something

- **procedures** --- the usual ways of doing something

- **take (measure)** --- to find the size of something

- **pressure** --- the power made by pushing sth. against sth. else

- **measure** --- to find the size of something

- **height** --- how tall something is

- **weight** --- how heavy something is

- **fortunate** --- lucky

- **hereditary** --- sth. a parent gives to a child before birth or after death

- **issues (problems)** --- worries

- **disease** --- when your body is sick

- **cancer** --- a serious disease where cells grow strangely and kill normal cells

- **diabetes** --- a disease where your body cannot control your blood sugar

- **arthritis** --- a disease where the places between bones hurts

- **current [adjective]** --- happening now

- **reply [verb]** --- to answer

- **medication** --- one or more medicines

- **examination** --- a very careful check of something

- **face to face** --- meeting someone in the same place

- **cure [verb]** --- to make a sick person healthy again

- **in no time** --- very quickly

- **go into detail** --- to explain everything about something

- **chest** --- the body part from the neck to stomach

- **occur** --- to happen

- **throughout** --- in every part

- **palpitations** --- a problem where your heart beats faster than normal

- **coughing** --- making air come out of your lungs very quickly

- **wheezing** --- breathing with difficulty and noise

- **place (move)** --- to put something in a place

- **stethoscope** --- a tool a doctor uses to check your heart and breathing

- **subtle** --- hard to notice

- **nods [noun]** --- moving the head up and down to show you agree

- **appear (look)** --- to seem

- **reach (a decision)** --- to decide

- **diagnosis** --- the naming of your disease after getting checked by a doctor

- **asthma** --- a condition that makes breathing difficult

- **common** --- happening often

- **develop (a problem)** --- to start to have a problem

- **inhaler** --- a tool you use to breathe in medicine

- **curb [verb]** --- to control a problem

- **require (be necessary)** --- to need

- **keep at bay** --- to control a problem

- **prescription** --- a written order from a doctor for a medicine

- **head (towards)** --- to go closer to something

- **pharmacy** --- a store that sells medicine

- **drop something off** --- to take something and leave it somewhere

- **customer service desk** --- the place you go to get help in a store

- **wander** --- to walk around slowly without trying to go to any place

- **fill a prescription** --- to prepare a medicine to take home

- **browse** --- to look around without trying to find anything

- **shelves** --- flat things on a wall or in a case that you can put stuff on

- **tons (many)** --- a lot

- **products** --- things made to sell

- **treat (an illness)** --- to give care to somebody

- **allergies** --- conditions that make you sick when you eat or touch sth.

- **flu** --- a disease that makes you very weak and hurt a lot

- **constipation** --- a condition that makes it hard to poo

- **diarrhea** --- an illness where you poo more often and mostly water

- **pharmacist** --- the person who prepares medicine at the pharmacy

- **call out (shout)** --- to get someone to look at you by talking loudly

- **pick up (hold)** --- take something

- **parking lot** --- a place where you leave your car

- **dose [noun]** --- the medicine taken at one time

- **instantly** --- immediately

- **significantly** --- in a large or important way

- **subside** --- to become weaker or calmer

- **grateful** --- a feeling of or showing thanks

- **miracle** --- a very lucky thing that happened that you cannot believe

- **ordeal** --- a very difficult event that hurts you badly

- **constant (not stopping)** --- never changing

- **state (condition)** --- how something is doing

- **quality of life** --- the level of health and happiness a person has

- **diet (nutrition)** --- the food you eat usually

- **improvements** --- things getting better

Comprehension Questions

1. What kind of smoker was John?
     A) He only smoked at social events.
     B) He smoked a pack a day.
     C) He was suffering from emphysema.
     D) He had never smoked a cigarette in his life.

2. How did John get rid of his splitting headache?
     A) The doctor cured him.
     B) He took pain relievers.
     C) He used his inhaler.
     D) The nurse massaged his forehead.

3. Which of the following is NOT considered a serious illness?
     A) Heart disease
     B) Coughing
     C) Diabetes
     D) Cancer

4. What tool does a doctor use to listen to the internal sounds of a human or animal body?
    A) Prescription
    B) Stethoscope
    C) Diagnosis
    D) Symptoms

5. What does an inhaler do?
    A) It keeps asthma symptoms at bay.
    B) It keeps asthma from spreading to other people.
    C) It keeps asthma from becoming cancer.
    D) It cures asthma altogether.

CHAPTER TWO:
FOOD

John had been on a **diet** now for four weeks and had already lost 12 **pounds**. His new diet was very **strict**, but he followed it **extremely** closely.

For breakfast, he ate a small bowl of **oatmeal** cooked in the **microwave** with either water or milk. He also had a **serving** of fruit with his oatmeal, like a banana, **strawberries**, or a **mango**. And of course, what breakfast would have been complete without a cup of coffee?

For lunch, John preferred to eat a light meal to **maximize** his weight **loss**, so he usually had a **spinach** salad. On top of his salad, he put carrots, onions, **cucumbers**, **croutons**, and **nuts**. **Dressing tends** to have a lot of **calories**, so he added just a small **dab**. If the salad did not fill him up, he also ate some soup. Usually, it was tomato soup, as that was his favorite.

For dinner, there were a few **options** available, **depending** on what he wanted that night. He could have a pasta and vegetable **mix** cooked in **olive** oil and Italian **spices**. Or he could have rice and beans **topped off** with a garlic and onion sauce. He could also have a Thai curry dish with **kale** and **sweet potato**. All **choices** required some cooking, but it **was worth it in the end**.

All was going pretty well for John until the fifth week started. Like many of us, he worked a **stressful** and **demanding** job, so there wasn't always enough time to prepare every meal. His **energy** started **dropping**, while his **appetite** and **hunger** started **rising rapidly**.

Soon, the small bowl of oatmeal for breakfast became the large bowl of sugary **cereal**. And the black coffee was now **drowned in** a high calorie coffee **creamer**.

The salad for lunch **turned into** fast food meals, since John was always **running late** for meetings. **Originally**, he was drinking water with this meal as well as every meal, but now it was **soda**.

And dinner was just **hopeless** after a while. John would come home **exhausted** from work and could not **bring himself to** cook. Pizza, ice cream, **french fries**, and snacks were much easier choices and helped **take his mind off** all the **anxiety**.

Several weeks later, he had **regained** all 12 pounds he had lost and even gained an **additional** 10 pounds **on top of** that! The **failure** made John feel even worse. He **vowed**, for his next diet, that he would be even more strict and eat even less food.

Unfortunately, he didn't realize that the **massive** drop in calories was **causing** an **equally** massive **dip** in his energy levels and **increased cravings** for **junk food**. It would take many **attempts** before he finally learned that starting his diet with lots of healthy foods and slowly **cutting down** calories would be the **wiser** move.

Vocabulary

• **diet (weight loss)** --- eating less to lose weight

• **pounds (weight)** --- a number for weight in the US

• **strict (serious)** --- must be done exactly in some way

- **extremely** --- stronger than very

- **oatmeal** --- a soft, thick food that is usually eaten for breakfast

- **microwave [noun]** --- a tool that cooks food very quickly

- **serving [noun]** --- the food you give to one person for one meal

- **strawberries** --- small red fruits with a green top

- **mango** --- a red, yellow, and green fruit with an orange inside

- **maximize** --- to make something as big as you can

- **loss** --- losing something or having less of something

- **spinach** --- a vegetable with big dark green leaves

- **cucumbers** --- long dark green vegetables with a light green inside

- **croutons** --- small pieces of toasted bread used in soups and salads

- **nuts** --- small dry fruits with a hard case on the outside

- **dressing** --- a sauce you put on salads

- **tend (be likely)** --- to be true usually

- **calories** --- a number for how much energy is in a food

- **dab [noun]** --- a little bit

- **options** --- possible things you can do

- **depend (be controlled by)** --- to be decided by sth.

- **mix [noun]** --- many things put together

- **olive** --- a small green or black fruit with a very hard center

- **spices** --- things from plants used to make food delicious

- **top off** --- to finish something by adding one final thing

- **kale** --- a green or purple vegetable with large leaves that are hard to eat

- **sweet potato** --- a sweet vegetable that looks likes a potato but isn't

- **choices** --- things you can choose

- **be worth it** --- good enough to put the time into doing

- **in the end** --- after carefully thinking about everything

- **stressful** --- makes you feel worried

- **demanding** --- difficult

- **energy** --- the power needed for work

- **drop (become less)** --- to go down

- **appetite** --- the feeling that you want food

- **hunger** --- the feeling that you need food

- **rise [verb]** --- to go up

- **rapidly** --- quickly

- **cereal (breakfast)** --- a food eaten with milk for breakfast

- **drown something in** --- to cover something in water or a liquid

- **creamer** --- a cream you can put into coffee

- **turn into** --- to become

- **run late** --- to be late

- **originally** --- at the beginning

- **soda** --- a sweet drink made with a special type of water

- **hopeless** --- without hope

- **exhausted** --- very tired

- **bring yourself to** --- to make yourself do something

- **french fries** --- long, thin pieces of potatoes cooked in oil

- **take your mind off** --- to stop thinking about something

- **anxiety** --- the feeling something bad is going to happen

- **regain** --- to get something back

- **additional** --- extra

- **on top of something** --- in addition to something

- **failure** --- when something has failed

- **vow [noun]** --- a very serious promise

- **massive** --- very large

- **cause** --- to make something happen

- **equally** --- in the same way

- **dip (a fall)** --- something becoming lower

- **increased [adjective]** --- larger

- **cravings** --- feelings of really wanting something

- **junk food** --- food that is bad for your health

- **attempts [noun]** --- tries at something difficult

- **cut down (on something)** --- to do less of something

- **wise** --- knowing a lot and can make good decisions

Comprehension Questions

1. How much dressing did John put on his salad?
   A) None at all
   B) A big glob
   C) A small dab
   D) He drowned it in dressing.

2. What was John's favorite meal for dinner?
   A) A pasta and vegetable mix cooked in olive oil and Italian spices
   B) Rice and beans topped with a garlic and onion sauce
   C) A Thai curry dish with kale and sweet potato
   D) The story does not say what John's favorite meal is.

3. What started happening during the fifth week of John's diet?
   A) His energy started rising, while his appetite and hunger started dropping rapidly.
   B) His energy started dropping, while his appetite and hunger started rising rapidly.
   C) His energy stayed the same, while his appetite and hunger started rising rapidly.
   D) His energy started dropping, while his appetite and hunger stayed the same.

4. Pizza, ice cream, french fries, and snacks are usually considered...
   A) healthy food.
   B) a well-balanced breakfast.
   C) junk food.
   D) low-calorie foods.

5. If John started his diet at 200 pounds, how many pounds did he weigh at the end of the story?
   A) 190 pounds
   B) 200 pounds
   C) 210 pounds
   D) 220 pounds

CHAPTER THREE:
EXERCISE

———

John decided that he should really start **taking** better **care of** himself by exercising. It would help **manage** his stress and even help him lose the extra weight he put on. Starting next week, he would begin a **jogging routine**, where he would run five days a week.

On the first day, he woke up extra early before work and put on his **tennis shoes, eager** to **get started**. After some **basic stretches**, the jogging started, and everything seemed to go well. **Within** two minutes, however, John was **out of breath**. He was wheezing, and his breathing became **super** heavy. And after just five minutes, the jogging was **replaced** by walking. While it would be easy to **blame** his asthma and **call it quits**, he **admitted** the **truth**. He was **out of shape**.

As time passed, days became weeks. Weeks became months. John was now able to run **continually** for 30 minutes. Within a year or two, he could be running a **marathon**, he thought. While he was **proud** of his improvement, doing **nothing but cardio** had **grown** extremely boring, so a change of routine was the next **step**.

John's friends Andy and Joe had invited him to come **lift weights** after work, so they all met at the gym, eager to spend some time together. They decided to **commit** to a **workout program** five days a week, where they would work one body part per week: chest, back, **shoulders**, legs, and arms.

Each day required **strenuous effort**, but the **endorphin rush** at the end of each workout made it all worth it. To **cool down**, the men relaxed by walking on the **treadmills** or **sweating it out** in the **sauna** for 10 minutes.

Some time passed, and John decided that weightlifting wasn't a good fit for him. Andy and Joe **got** too **competitive** with it, and the **intensity** of the workouts had become more **painful** than fun. At the gym, however, they offered yoga classes, so John **signed up**, eager to start.

The classes taught a **variety** of stretches and **poses designed** to **loosen** the body and **calm** the mind. The lessons were not easy **by any means**, and they made all the students sweat. Yet, it was not as **intense** as weightlifting. And it was much more fun and relaxing than jogging.

John left each class feeling **refreshed** and excited to come back for more. He even started chatting with some pretty girls **whom** he **looked forward to** seeing every week. It was a routine with an extra **incentive** to **maintain**.

Vocabulary

- **take care of (protect)** --- to keep something safe

- **manage (control)** --- to control something

- **jogging** --- running slowly

- **routine [noun]** --- the normal way you do things

- **tennis shoes** --- simple sports shoes

- **eager** --- very interested to do something

- **get started** --- to begin

- **basic** --- simple or important

- **stretches (body)** --- pulling parts of the body to relax or prepare it

- **within (time)** --- after a time starts and before it ends

- **out of breath** --- hard to breathe after exercise

- **super [adverb]** --- very

- **replace** --- to use something new instead of something old

- **blame [verb]** --- to think sth. is the reason why sth. is bad

- **call it quits** --- *(informal)* to stop

- **admit (say)** --- to say something is true

- **truth** --- a true fact

- **out of shape (person)** --- not in good condition

- **continually** --- in a way that repeats

- **marathon** --- a very long race

- **proud** --- feeling happy about what somebody has or has done

- **nothing but** --- only

- **cardio** --- exercise to make your heart work harder

- **grow (begin)** --- to become

- **step (part)** --- one smaller thing you do to do something bigger

- **lift weights** --- to pick up heavy things as a way to exercise

- **commit (promise)** --- to promise to do sth.

- **workout program** --- an exercise plan

- **shoulders** --- parts of the body between the arms and the neck

- **strenuous** --- needing a lot of energy and work to do

- **effort** --- energy or work that is done on something

- **endorphin rush** --- the very good feeling you get after exercise or stress

- **cool down (exercise)** --- to exercise a little after doing a lot

- **treadmills** --- exercise machines that you walk and run on

- **sweat [verb]** --- to pass water through your skin

- **sweat it out (exercise)** --- to make the body work hard and sweat

- **sauna** --- a very hot room you go into to sweat

- **get (become)** --- to start to be

- **competitive** --- trying very hard to win

- **intensity** --- the level of something

- **painful** --- something that hurts

- **sign up** --- to agree to join something

- **variety** --- one or many kinds of something

- **poses** --- putting the body in many special ways for reasons

- **design [verb]** --- to think, plan, and make something

- **loosen** --- to become easier to move

- **calm [verb]** --- to make someone become quiet and relaxed

- **by any means** --- in any possible way

- **intense** --- feeling a lot of something

- **refreshed** --- feeling less tired and more relaxed

- **whom** --- the object form of "who"

- **look forward to** --- to feel excited about something in the future

- **incentive** --- something that makes you want to do something

- **maintain** --- to keep something at the same level

Comprehension Questions

1. What kind of shoes did John run in?
   A) Cleats
   B) Tennis shoes
   C) High heels
   D) Running boots

2. Why did John stop running?
   A) He accomplished his goal.
   B) He was tired of getting up early.
   C) He was extremely bored.
   D) He didn't want to run a marathon.

3. John, Andy, and Joe committed to a workout program that focused on...
   A) chest, back, shoulders, legs, and arms.
   B) chest, back, running, legs, and cardio.
   C) chest, swimming, shoulders, running, and arms.
   D) yoga, cardio, jogging, weightlifting, and sports.

4. How did the men relax after working out?

    A) They ran on the treadmills while listening to music.

    B) They did a quick 10-minute yoga routine.

    C) They swam in the pool or took a hot shower.

    D) They walked on the treadmills or sweated it out in the sauna for 10 minutes.

5. Why did John stop lifting weights?

    A) He was extremely bored.

    B) The workouts were too intense and competitive.

    C) Andy and Joe quit lifting.

    D) John suffered an injury.

CHAPTER FOUR:
HOBBIES

"It would be really nice to **go on a date** with one of those girls from class," John thought to himself. "**Hopefully**, I can find something **in common** with one of them and maybe make a **connection**."

His hobbies were **somewhat relatable**. Everybody liked watching TV and movies, including John, but would he be able to find a girl who liked video games? If not, could he find someone who **was into professional** baseball and basketball as much as he was? It would be amazing if he had someone to talk to about **politics**, history, and **government**.

The first girl he met from yoga class was Jenny, who seemed really smart **right away**. She was a big **reader**, but of **fiction rather than non-fiction**. Her **passion** was **literature**, and she could talk for hours about the current story she was reading. **Besides** that, she spent a lot of time taking care of her dog and taking him for long walks. And **occasionally**, she'd **treat herself** to a bottle of wine and watch **horror movies**.

Emily was the second girl he **got to know** from class, **although** she didn't always have a lot of time to talk. There was always somewhere she needed to be. It was **obvious** that she was extremely fit and **in** great **shape**, and John later learned that she was a **female bodybuilding athlete** and **coach**. If she didn't have an appointment with a **client**, she was busy building her business. Emily had a big **social media following** and built a clothing **brand** that sold T-shirts, **sweatshirts**, hats, and **accessories**. You could say she was a **workaholic**, but you had to admit she was very **successful**.

The last girl John spent time with was Jessica, who was a bit of a **social butterfly**. She had a large **social circle** of friends to talk to and **hang out** with. It was clear that she was an **extrovert**. If she wasn't **texting**, she was out with friends, drinking and **clubbing**. On the occasion that she did decide to stay home, Jessica would watch Japanese anime and play video games.

John was immediately **drawn** to Jessica, as he had finally found someone he could **nerd out** with about current and **upcoming** games. Their **personalities**, however, didn't seem to **match** very well. The **chemistry** just wasn't there. They never seemed to be able to talk about anything **outside of** their **mutual** hobby.

Emily never really had much time to talk, but Jenny was more than **willing** to spend some time together with him. John listened to her talk about all her favorite books, and she even **convinced** him to try reading a book **via audiobooks**. Jenny didn't show much **interest** in sports or history, but she was **attracted** to the passion and energy John **emitted whenever** he spoke about **subjects** he cared about. Their mutual interest in **one another** was enough for them to start dating.

Vocabulary

- **go on a date** --- to meet with sb. who is or could become a girl/boyfriend

- **hopefully** --- used to say what you want to happen

- **in common** --- shared with something else

- **connection** --- joining two or more things together

- **somewhat** --- to some level

- **relatable (to sb.)** --- makes you feel you can understand sth.

- **be into something** --- to like something

- **professional [adjective]** --- something done at a very high level

- **politics** --- the business of controlling a group or a place

- **government** --- the group of people who control a country

- **right away** --- immediately

- **reader** --- someone who reads

- **fiction** --- a story that is created and not real

- **rather than** --- instead of

- **non-fiction** --- writing that is about real things and people

- **passion** --- a very strong feeling of liking or hating something

- **literature** --- something written at a very high level

- **besides** --- in addition to

- **occasionally** --- once in a while

- **treat somebody (pay for)** --- to buy sth. nice for somebody

- **horror movies** --- scary movies

- **get to know** --- to spend time with sb. and learn about them

- **although** --- while, but

- **obvious** --- easy to see or understand

- **in ... shape** --- in ... condition

- **female** --- about girls and women

- **bodybuilding** --- a sport where you try to look big and strong

- **athlete** --- a person who is very good at sports and exercise

- **coach [noun]** --- a person who helps people improve at sth.

- **client** --- a customer who buys high level things

- **social media** --- places on the internet where people talk

- **following (people)** --- a group of people who really like sth.

- **brand (business)** --- something with a name sold by a company

- **sweatshirts** --- thick shirts with long arms

- **accessories (extra)** --- things added because they look nice or are useful

- **workaholic** --- someone who cannot stop working

- **successful** --- something that does something right

- **social butterfly** --- someone who is friendly with everyone

- **social circle** --- a group of people who know and talk to each other

- **hang out** --- to spend time at a place or with people

- **extrovert** --- someone who gets energy from being around people

- **texting** --- messaging people from your cellphone

- **clubbing** --- going to places in the evening to drink and dance

- **draw (attention)** --- to make people look at you

- **nerd out** --- to get excited about something not usually popular

- **upcoming** --- happening soon

- **personalities** --- the kinds of people someone can be

- **match (mix well)** --- to fit together

- **chemistry (people)** --- the way two people talk to each other

- **outside of** --- except for

- **mutual** --- shared by two or more people

- **willing** --- ready to do something

- **convince** --- to make somebody do or believe something

- **via** --- through

- **audiobooks** --- recorded books that you listen to

- **interest (feeling)** --- wanting to know more about sth.

- **attract** --- to make somebody interested in something

- **emit** --- to send out energy

- **whenever** --- any or every time

- **subjects (conversation)** --- things that are being talked about

- **one another** --- each other

Comprehension Questions

1. If you have something in common with somebody, it means that...

    A) you both like each other.

    B) you are in love with each other.

    C) you do not like each other.

    D) you have a mutual hobby you are both interested in.

2. Politics, history, and government are typically considered...

    A) fiction.

    B) non-fiction.

    C) literature.

    D) All of the above

3. Emily was not only a female bodybuilding athlete and coach but also...

    A) a private business owner.

    B) an alcoholic.

    C) a yoga instructor.

    D) a social butterfly.

4. Which of the following best describes an extrovert?

    A) Someone who is loud and annoying

    B) Someone who is bold and daring

    C) Someone who is talkative and outgoing

    D) Someone who is shy and reserved

5. Which couple had the best chemistry in the end?
    A) John and Jessica
    B) John and Emily
    C) John and Jenny
    D) John and the yoga instructor

CHAPTER FIVE:
WORK

While John's **social life** was **blooming**, his life at work was the **polar opposite**. He worked at an office for an **insurance** company, and while the pay was good, the **workload** was **overwhelming**.

Each morning, he checked his work email to find 50 new **requests** that had to be immediately **dealt with**. If he didn't quickly **process** and **dispatch** the emails before lunch, he would **get caught behind schedule** and most **likely** have to work **overtime**. It was extremely stressful and **more so** when his boss was watching him over his shoulder.

John's boss had to be strict with all the **employees**. One mistake and it could **cost** the company **a small fortune**. Not only would the employee be **disciplined harshly**, but the boss would be too.

Insurance was a difficult business to work in. It was not for the weak. Meetings, **documents**, and **regulations** were all of the **utmost importance**, and you could not **afford** to miss or forget anything. You could be **fired** for it!

"How am I going to **make it** to **retirement**?" John asked himself at least once a week. And he was lucky if this question only **came up** once that week. Stress and anxiety were **pushing him to his limits**. It **was only a matter of time** before he broke.

What would life have been like had he chosen a different college **degree**? What if he **went into computer science**? Would he have enjoyed **programming** more? What if he **pushed** himself harder while playing for the college baseball team? Would he have made it to the professional level? What if he had made it as a **pro-gamer** back in high school and **got to** play video games **for a living**? It would have been **a dream come true**.

Life didn't **turn out** that way for John, unfortunately. He might **have been stuck with** a job he hated, but at least he had hope things would change. Many of his **co-workers** seemed to **lack** that same hope. **Depression** and anxiety were common in his workplace, but there were a **handful** of **colleagues** who were fun to talk to and **crack jokes** with to **lighten the mood**. They made it just a little easier to **get through** each day. That **made all the difference**.

There were others, **though**, who seemed to be **absolutely crushed** by the harshness of life and were now just **shells of their former selves**. Those people scared John more than any boss ever had.

But when would things change? How would they change? The only thing that was **certain** was that something must change.

Vocabulary

• **social life** --- things you do with other people when not working

• **bloom (grow)** --- to grow and become healthy

• **polar opposite** --- completely different

• **insurance** --- paying a company to help you later

• **workload** --- how much work there is

- **overwhelming** --- feeling too much of something

- **requests [noun]** --- *(formal)* things you ask for

- **deal with** --- to find an answer to a problem

- **process (information)** --- to deal with information

- **dispatch** --- *(formal)* to send

- **get caught behind schedule** --- to be late

- **likely** --- probably

- **overtime** --- extra time you work

- **more so** --- especially

- **employees** --- people that are paid to work for other people

- **cost a small fortune** --- to be very expensive

- **discipline (punish)** --- to make sb. feel bad because they did sth. wrong

- **harshly** --- in a way that is not kind or is too strong

- **documents** --- written information put on papers or a computer

- **regulations** --- rules made by people who have power

- **utmost** --- most extreme

- **importance** --- how important something is

- **afford (have enough)** --- to have the time or money to do sth.

- **fire (from a job)** --- to make somebody leave their job

- **make it (survive)** --- to deal with a difficult time until it ends

- **retirement** --- when you stop working jobs for all time

- **come up (appear)** --- to happen

- **push sth. to the limit** --- to go until sth. cannot go anymore

- **be only a matter of time** --- used when you think sth. will happen

- **degree (school)** --- a special paper given to you after you finish school

- **go into (start)** --- to begin

- **computer science** --- the study of computers

- **programming** --- writing computer programs

- **push (work hard)** --- to make someone work hard

- **pro-gamer** --- a person who plays video games professionally

- **get to do sth. (chance)** --- to have the chance to do sth.

- **for a living** --- as your job

- **a dream come true** --- a dream that has become real

- **turn out (happen)** --- to happen in a special way

- **be stuck with sth.** --- to have to be with sth. you don't want

- **co-workers** --- people you work with

- **lack** --- to not have

- **depression (sadness)** --- when sb. feels very unhappy for a long time

- **handful (few)** --- a small number of things

- **colleagues** --- people you work with

- **crack jokes** --- to make jokes

- **lighten the mood** --- to make people be less serious

- **get through something (complete)** --- to finish something hard

- **make all the difference** --- to be very important

- **though** --- while, but

- **absolutely** --- in every way

- **crush (shock)** --- to make somebody feel sad and surprised

- **shells of their former selves** --- things that are much worse than before

- **certain (believe)** --- strongly believing something is true

Comprehension Questions

1. What would happen if John didn't quickly dispatch and process the emails before lunch?
   A) He would be fired and sent home immediately.
   B) He would get to go home early and play video games on his computer.
   C) He wouldn't be eligible for a promotion for the next five years.
   D) He would get caught behind schedule and most likely have to work overtime.

2. Who could potentially be disciplined for a mistake at the office?
   A) The employee
   B) The boss
   C) The employee and the boss
   D) Only John

3. Throughout his life, John had considered multiple career paths but not...

   A) teaching at a high school.

   B) becoming a pro-gamer.

   C) playing baseball at the professional level.

   D) becoming a computer programmer.

4. A colleague is another word for...

   A) a boss.

   B) a friend.

   C) a supervisor.

   D) a co-worker.

5. Those who are crushed by the harshness of life are most likely experiencing...

   A) an upset stomach.

   B) depression and anxiety.

   C) dreams coming true.

   D) a lightening of the mood.

CHAPTER SIX:
ANIMALS AND NATURE

To **relieve** some of the stress and anxiety he had been **accumulating** for quite some time, John **set off** on a nature walk. He heard that spending a day or two in the mountains would **do wonders for him** and his **mental** health. The **isolation** would give his mind time and space to **detox** and refresh. Animals would be his only **companions** during the walk.

His home was **located** in an apartment **complex,** so it was pretty **rare** to see any **wildlife** besides the occasional **squirrel. Groundhogs** and **foxes** were even rarer **sights.** Because he spent all his time **indoors,** he mostly saw **spiders** and **house centipedes.** He **was** not **particularly fond of the latter.**

It was not too long of a drive to reach the mountains since the town he lived in was near a **mountain range.** Upon parking and exiting his **vehicle,** he **was** immediately **greeted by** a few **deer grazing** in an **open** field. They slowly **picked at** the grass and **wagged** their **tails,** not **paying** much **attention** to John. Then, **suddenly,** a large **booming** sound from far away caused them to **scatter frantically.** It was the sound of a **gunshot. Hunting season** must have started.

John was **unsure** where to begin **hiking,** but his question was answered when he saw some other **hikers** walking towards an **opening** in the **forest.** And **what a** beautiful forest it was! The **evergreen** trees and sun **shining** through them made for some

breathtaking scenery. The **lake** added to the **vastness** of the place, and a feeling of smallness **struck** John from deep **within**.

He could see the life **flowing** through every little **bush, insect,** and bird he **came across.** A **peaceful harmony** could be felt **in the air.** Sure, there were bears and **mountain lions** far up somewhere in the mountains, but they too were part of the **ecosystem** that connected all life in the forest. The **frogs** on the **lakeshore** had just as much life as the **beavers** building **dams.** They might have been different **creatures,** but they were both small **fragments** from the same world. They were made from the same **chemical elements** found scattered throughout the **universe.**

As the sun was **setting,** it became less and less safe to **remain** in the forest. It would be better to avoid nighttime **predators,** so John hiked back to his car. Exhausted from the **journey,** he sat in his car wondering about the next time he would come back. There would **definitely** be a next time, and it would definitely have to be with Jenny.

Vocabulary

• **relieve (make better)** --- to make a problem not as bad

• **accumulate** --- to get or grow more of something over time

• **set off** --- to start

• **do wonders for sth.** --- to be very good for sth.

• **mental** --- about the mind

• **isolation** --- being alone

- **detox [verb]** --- to stop taking in unhealthy things for some time
- **companions** --- people or animals you spend a lot of time with
- **locate (be)** --- to be somewhere
- **complex (building)** --- a large building or a group of buildings
- **rare (not often)** --- very unusual
- **wildlife** --- animals and plants living in nature
- **squirrel** --- a small animal that eats nuts and lives in trees
- **groundhogs** --- animals that are like big squirrels but live in the ground
- **foxes** --- animals that are like dogs but are usually red and brown
- **sights (views)** --- things that you can see
- **indoors** --- inside a building
- **spiders** --- very small animals with eight legs
- **house centipedes** --- very small, long animals with very many legs
- **be fond of** --- to like something
- **particularly** --- especially
- **the latter** --- the second of two things said
- **mountain range** --- a group of mountains
- **vehicle (machine)** --- a machine that you can drive
- **be greeted by** --- to be the first thing you see, hear, or smell somewhere
- **deer** --- large animals with four long legs that eat grass and run fast
- **graze (eat grass)** --- to (make animals) eat grass in a field

- **open (no covering)** --- not covered

- **pick at (eat)** --- to eat slowly when you are not hungry

- **wag** --- to move a finger or tail side to side several times

- **tails** --- the long part of animals' bodies that come out at the back

- **pay attention** --- to watch or listen very carefully

- **suddenly** --- surprisingly quickly

- **booming (sound)** --- making a loud and deep sound

- **scatter (move)** --- to (make things) move away from each other

- **frantically** --- quickly but not calmly

- **gunshot** --- when a small thing comes out of a gun very, very fast

- **hunting season** --- a time when some animals in nature can be killed

- **unsure** --- not sure

- **hiking** --- going on long walks in nature

- **hikers** --- people who go on long walks in nature

- **opening (space)** --- a space where something can go through

- **forest** --- a large place that is covered with trees

- **what a ...** --- used when you have a strong feeling about sth.

- **evergreen** --- a plant that always has green leaves

- **shine (light)** --- to send out light

- **breathtaking** --- very exciting, beautiful, or surprising

- **scenery (nature)** --- the look of nature

- **lake** --- a large, deep place of water smaller than an ocean or sea

- **vastness** --- the very, very large size of something

- **strike (feel)** --- to come into your mind quickly and as a surprise

- **within (space)** --- inside

- **flow (move)** --- to move like water in a river

- **bush (plant)** --- a thick, short, and round plant

- **insect** --- a very small animal with six legs and three body parts

- **come across (find)** --- to find or meet something by luck

- **peaceful** --- calm and quiet

- **harmony (feeling)** --- when everyone feels good being together

- **in the air** --- used when you feel something strongly

- **mountain lions** --- large cats that live mostly in America

- **ecosystem** --- a large group of things living together in one place

- **frogs** --- small animals that live in and out of water and can jump

- **lakeshore** --- the ground next to a lake

- **beavers** --- brown animals with big tails and large teeth

- **dams** --- walls made to stop moving water

- **creatures** --- living animals

- **fragments** --- small pieces of something

- **chemical elements** --- the 118 different atoms found in the universe

- **universe** --- everything in space

- **set (sun)** --- to go below the sky and ground

- **remain (stay)** --- to stay in the same place or the same way

- **predators** --- animals that eat other animals

- **journey (trip)** --- a long trip

- **definitely** --- certainly

Comprehension Questions

1. Where did John go for his nature walk?
    A) Under the mountains
    B) Inside the mountains
    C) On the mountains
    D) In the mountains

2. Which wildlife animal did John NOT see around his apartment?
    A) Squirrels
    B) Bears
    C) Groundhogs
    D) Foxes

3. What were the deer doing in the open field?
    A) Rolling their eyes
    B) Grazing
    C) Shooting guns
    D)Hunting smaller animals

4. How did the forest make John feel?

    A) The vastness of the area made John feel small.

    B) The openness of the area made John feel exhausted.

    C) The vagueness of the area made John feel anxious.

    D) The smallness of the area made John feel vast.

5. According to John, how was all life connected in the forest?

    A) It was all getting demolished by bulldozers.

    B) It was all fair game for hunters.

    C) It was all one ecosystem that lived in peaceful harmony.

    D) It was all good for relieving his stress and anxiety.

CHAPTER SEVEN:
TOWN AND CITY

Before his big date with Jenny today, John had a few **errands** to **run** to make sure everything was ready. First of all, a trip to the bank was needed, so he could **withdraw** enough cash for the busy day ahead. Along the way to the bank, he stopped by his favorite coffee shop to pick up some much-needed **caffeine** to **jump-start** the day.

Next, he had to **make a run** to the post office and drop off some mail that was **overdue** and nearly late. After that, it **was off to** the **mall** to find a new **outfit** to wear on today's date. He **perused** two **clothing** stores and even had enough time to **get** himself a new haircut at the **barber shop**.

At 2:00 pm, John and Jenny **met up**, ready to take a tour around town. They started by walking around the park, **catching up** on what happened with each other during the week. Inside the park was a large **plaza**, where the couple found a small concert being **performed** by a rock band. After hearing a few songs, they left the park and drove towards a **local amusement park**.

Due to a large accident, the amusement park had to be **shut down**, so as a **back-up** plan, the couple decided to go to the movie theater instead. To Jenny's luck, they were able to find a horror movie playing that week. It would be an hour-long wait for the movie, so they grabbed an early dinner at a **nearby** Mexican restaurant with just enough time to **make it** back to the theater.

The movie turned out to be **fairly generic** and **predictable**, but there was one **jumpscare** that **got** both John and Jenny really, really good.

As the evening came, the couple had a mutual feeling of not wanting to **stay out** too late in the city, but they agreed to have one drink at a **unique** bar they found searching on their smartphones. It had a **medieval castle theme** and was **decorated** with **banners**, suits of **armor**, and chairs that looked like **thrones**. The conversation **picked up** between the two and along with it came more drinking.

Now they were both too **intoxicated** to drive home safely! Not **feeling up for** a night of clubbing, they would wait two hours to **sober up** before driving home. Calling a taxi would be a crazy expensive **option**, and it wasn't all that much of a wait to begin with. To **pass the time**, they walked along the **boardwalk** and stopped by the **convenience store** for a quick snack.

John and Jenny **thoroughly** enjoyed each other's **presence**, so the hours passed quicker than expected, but it was time to **part ways**. A **brief** kiss was shared, along with a couple of **cheeky smiles**, and **that was it** before they both drove home.

Vocabulary

- **errands** --- short trips you make to do small things

- **run (business)** --- to do or manage

- **withdraw (money)** --- to take your money out of the bank

- **caffeine** --- a drug found inside of coffee and tea

- **jump-start (quick start)** --- to start something very quickly

- **make a run (move)** --- to run to something in a hurry

- **overdue** --- late

- **be off to** --- to go away to somewhere

- **mall (shopping)** --- a very large building with many stores

- **outfit** --- a group of clothes worn at one time

- **peruse** --- to read or look at something carefully

- **clothing** --- clothes

- **get (something done)** --- to make something happen

- **barber shop (hair)** --- a place where boys and men get haircuts

- **meet up** --- to meet somebody to do something together

- **catch up (find out)** --- to learn about things that have happened

- **plaza** --- a large, open outdoor place in a town

- **perform** --- to sing, dance, act, or play music for people

- **local [adjective]** --- from the place that is being talked about

- **amusement park** --- a large park with rides, games, shows, and food

- **shut down** --- to stop something from working

- **back-up** --- something prepared in case something else fails

- **nearby** --- near *(as an adjective or adverb)*

- **make it (in time)** --- to get to a place before you are too late

- **fairly (kind of)** --- a bit

- **generic (art)** --- neither special nor interesting

- **predictable** --- easy to know what will happen

- **jumpscare** --- something so scary that it makes you jump

- **get (feel)** --- to make somebody feel something strongly

- **stay out** --- to be away from your house at night

- **unique** --- the only one like this

- **medieval** --- a time in history around 476-1453 AD

- **castle** --- a very large, strong, and tall building for kings and queens

- **theme** --- an idea that is found everywhere in something

- **decorate (art)** --- to make sth. look nice by putting things on it

- **banners** --- long pieces of cloth with a message or picture on them

- **armor** --- a very strong covering you wear in a fight

- **thrones** --- special chairs for kings and queens

- **pick up (increase)** --- to become larger

- **intoxicated (drug)** --- losing control of yourself because of a drug

- **feel up for something** --- to want to do something

- **sober up** --- to wait until you aren't drunk anymore

- **option (choice)** --- something you can choose

- **pass the time** --- to do something while you are waiting

- **boardwalk** --- a path made of wood

- **convenience store** --- a small shop that is open late

- **thoroughly (completely)** --- very much

- **presence (being)** --- being in a place

- **part ways (say goodbye)** --- to leave somebody

- **brief** --- short

- **cheeky smiles** --- faces that are both happy and funny

- **that was it** --- used to say something is finished

Comprehension Questions

1. When you put money into your bank account, it's called...
    A) withdrawing.
    B) checking your balance.
    C) opening your account.
    D) depositing.

2. What did John do at the mall?
    A) He played video games at the arcade.
    B) He hung out with friends and shopped for clothes.
    C) He shopped for clothes and got a haircut.
    D) He got a haircut and grabbed lunch at the food court.

3. Where did John and Jenny head towards immediately after leaving the park?
    A) The amusement park
    B) Home
    C) The movie theater
    D) The restaurant

4. How did the couple find out about the medieval-themed bar?

    A) They walked around looking for a bar.

    B) A mutual friend recommended it to them.

    C) They searched for nearby bars using their smartphones.

    D) They saw an advertisement for the bar.

5. If you are intoxicated, then it is unsafe to...

    A) drink more.

    B) drive a car.

    C) talk on the phone.

    D) walk around in public.

CHAPTER EIGHT:
STAYING AT HOME

I t was a Sunday afternoon. John had no **particular** plans, so he **slept in** and **allowed** himself to **catch up on** sleep he had missed during the week. It would not be a completely lazy day though, for he had **a number of household chores** to do.

Perhaps most important of all were the **unpaid** bills that needed to be **taken care of. Housing** wasn't free, **after all. Rent, electricity**, water, internet, **student loans**, and **phone plans** all had **payments due. Thanks to technology**, however, all of these could be paid **online** without leaving the house.

Next, the **laundry** had **piled up over** the week, and a **load** or two would be **necessary** for the **upcoming** week. He never **bothered** to **sort** his laundry into whites, darks, and colors; instead, he would just throw in as much as he could each load, **pour** in some laundry **detergent** and **fabric softener**, and **run** the laundry machine.

While he waited for each load to finish, he **figured** he would stay **productive** by **doing the dishes** and **vacuuming** the house. John's house was **by no means spotless**, but he did just a little bit each week to maintain what he could. This week, he would do some extra work in the kitchen. He **cleaned out** the **fridge** by **throwing away expired** foods. He also **scrubbed** the **counters** with **disinfectant** and **brushed off** all food **crumbs** to the floor. And he finished by **sweeping** the floor with his **broom** and **dustpan**. **Mopping** could wait another week, he thought.

John was more interested in spending the rest of his day at the computer playing video games. He was a fan of **strategy** games and could spend hours **coming up with** new strategies to **try out** against his friends online and even in single player games. When he needed a break, he would occasionally **get up** for a quick stretch, **peer** out the windows, **heat up** some food in the microwave, and sit back down for more **gaming**.

After spending too many hours in front of the computer, a small **existential crisis** would occur. Was it really all that wise to spend so much time gaming when it could be used for something more **meaningful**? Sure, there were videos he could watch online, but would that be any different? And so, he picked up the **headphones** in his bedroom and started to listen to some of the audiobook **recommended** to him by Jenny.

Listening to the book instantly felt like the right use of his time and even **opened up** the **opportunity** for some **self-reflection**. As he kept listening, he wandered around his house. He opened and closed his **closet** doors for no particular reason. He put his hand on the **couch** and let it **glide** over as he walked across. There was no dining room table to repeat this action, as he lived by himself and usually ate in the kitchen or out on the **balcony**.

Before he knew it, it was 10:00 pm. It was time for bed. While he didn't finish the audiobook, he certainly had something new to talk about next weekend when he would go to the family **gathering**. He could even bring Jenny and **introduce** her as the one who introduced him to the book.

Vocabulary

- **particular (special)** --- this one and no other

- **sleep in** --- to sleep more than usual

- **allow (let)** --- to let something do something

- **catch up on sth.** --- to do sth. you didn't do earlier

- **a number of** --- some

- **household chores** --- cooking and cleaning jobs done at home

- **unpaid** --- has not been paid

- **take care of (manage)** --- to find an answer to a problem

- **housing** --- houses

- **after all** --- used to give a reason for something

- **rent** --- the money you pay every month to use a place

- **electricity** --- energy that gives power to lights and machines

- **student loans** --- college students borrowing money from a bank

- **phone plans** --- the money people pay every month for phone service

- **payments due** --- money that you have to pay now

- **thanks to** --- because of something

- **technology** --- using science to make things

- **online (internet)** --- on the internet

- **laundry** --- clothes, towels, and sheets that need to be washed and dried

- **pile up** --- to become larger

- **over (during)** --- during something

- **load (something carried)** --- something carried at one time

- **necessary** --- needed

- **upcoming** --- happening soon

- **bother (make an effort)** --- to take time to do something

- **sort** --- to put things in a special order

- **pour** --- to make sth. come out of a sth. by moving one side down

- **detergent** --- something that cleans things like clothes and dishes

- **fabric softener** --- sth. you put in the laundry machine to make clothes softer

- **run (machine)** --- to use a machine

- **figure (expect)** --- to think

- **productive** --- doing a lot

- **do the dishes** --- to wash the dirty dishes

- **vacuum [verb]** --- to use a loud machine *(a vacuum)* to pick up dirt

- **by no means** --- not at all

- **spotless** --- very, very clean

- **clean out something** --- to clean something completely

- **fridge** --- *(same as refrigerator)* a machine to keep food cold

- **throw away** --- to put something in the garbage

- **expired (food)** --- food that shouldn't be eaten anymore

- **scrub** --- to clean something by rubbing it hard with something

- **counters (tables)** --- tables that are higher and can't be moved

- **disinfectant** --- something you clean with that kills germs

- **brush off** --- to take something off using a brush or your hand

- **crumbs** --- very small pieces of food

- **sweep** --- to clean the floor using a long brush

- **broom** --- a long brush you use to clean the floor

- **dustpan** --- a thing you brush dirt into from the floor

- **mop [verb]** --- to wash floors using a tool *(a mop)*

- **strategy** --- a large plan made of many smaller plans

- **come up with (think)** --- to think of an idea

- **try out something** --- to test something to see how good it is

- **get up** --- to stand up

- **peer [verb]** --- to look carefully

- **heat up something** --- to make something warm or hot

- **gaming** --- playing video games

- **existential crisis** --- thinking about if your life has any purpose

- **meaningful** --- useful or important

- **headphones** --- a machine you put on your ears to listen to things

- **recommended [adjective]** --- sb. said it was good enough to try

- **open up sth. (make available)** --- to make sth. available

- **opportunity** --- a time when something can happen

- **self-reflection** --- deep thinking about your feelings and actions

- **closet** --- a small room where you put clothes and other things

- **couch** --- a long, soft seat with a back for two or more people

- **glide (move)** --- to move easily with very little work

- **balcony** --- a place in a building that is upstairs, outside, and has walls

- **before someone knows it** --- surprisingly quickly

- **gathering** --- a meeting for many people

- **introduce (people)** --- to make people meet other people

Comprehension Questions

1. If someone needs to catch up on sleep, it means that...
    A) they have been sleeping too much.
    B) they have been sleeping too little.
    C) they enjoy sleeping.
    D) they have trouble falling asleep.

2. Which of the following is not considered a housing utility?
    A) Student loans
    B) Water
    C) Electricity
    D) Internet

3. When cleaning the kitchen, John did not...
    A) scrub the counters with disinfectant.
    B) throw away expired foods.
    C) mop the floor.
    D) sweep the floor with his broom and dustpan.

4. What's generally the fastest way to cook food?
    A) The stove
    B) The microwave
    C) The oven
    D) The toaster oven

5. Where did John find his headphones?
    A) In his bedroom
    B) In his closet
    C) In the laundry machine
    D) In the living room

CHAPTER NINE:
FAMILY AND OCCUPATIONS

Jenny happily agreed to **accompany** John on his visit to his family gathering the following weekend. They were now **officially** a couple, and it would be a good time to introduce her to his mother, father, and brothers.

Also at the **get-together** was John's uncle, named Doug. Doug was a **mechanical engineer** who worked on all kinds of machines, including **steam** and gas **turbines** and **electric generators**. He was an extremely **intelligent** man who helped **guide** John in his younger years.

While chatting with his uncle, he noticed his two cousins Michael and Joanne in the **background**. The three of them hung out quite **frequently** as kids and shared a lot of **childhood** memories. They **grew apart** as they got older, unfortunately, and **lost contact** with one another as they **entered** the **workforce**. Michael **ended up working his way up** to a **management position** at a **retail** store. And Joanne was a **part-time hairdresser** but a **full-time** mom.

Jenny was obviously **overwhelmed** by all the **new faces**, but she was able to get to know at least one person at the event. This person was John's **sister-in-law** Olivia. From the very **get-go**, the two **hit it off** and **established** an instant **rapport**. Jenny was a **journalist** by **trade**, and Olivia was a writer for a TV show that was **produced** by the same **media** company they both worked for.

While they had seen each other around the office, they had never met until now.

In the end, there were just too many people for Jenny to meet and even for John to catch up with. They briefly said hello to his grandmother and aunts, but they never got the chance to **greet** his **nieces** and **nephews**. All the kids were busy playing together in the **backyard**.

The family was able to take a group photo, which **included** Jenny, who was invited to join in. Every year, it was John's dad who was given the **task** to create the best family photo possible. **Leaving** the task to him made sense, given that he was a professional **photographer**.

The sun started going down, and the day was **growing late**. As everyone was leaving, John had another opportunity to speak with his Uncle Doug. He **voiced** his **concerns** about **burning out** at his current job at the insurance company and was **considering** a few possible paths he could take. Uncle Doug **advised** him that, even though he was not sure where he wanted to work in the future, he should definitely start taking classes as soon as possible. Waiting to start was the worst thing he could possibly do.

Vocabulary

• **occupations (work)** --- jobs

• **accompany (travel with)** --- to go somewhere with something

• **officially (formally)** --- in a way that everyone knows

• **get-together** --- a party

• **mechanical engineer** --- sb. who studies and builds machines

- **steam** --- hot gas made of water

- **turbines** --- machines that make power using liquids and a wheel

- **electric generators** --- machines that make electricity

- **intelligent** --- smart

- **guide (help)** --- to show someone how to do something hard

- **background (position)** --- things you see or hear behind other things

- **frequently** --- often

- **childhood** --- the time when you were a child

- **grow apart** --- to stop being close with someone over time

- **lose contact** --- to stop talking to someone you were close with

- **enter (as a member)** --- to become a member of something

- **workforce** --- the people who are available for work

- **end up** --- to reach a place or situation after a long time

- **work your way up** --- to work until you get a better job

- **management (people)** --- the people who control a business

- **position (work)** --- a job

- **retail** --- selling things to people in a store

- **part-time** --- done for only a part of a full work week

- **hairdresser** --- a person who cuts hair and makes it look nice

- **full-time** --- done for the whole work week

- **overwhelm (feel)** --- to make someone feel too much of sth.

- **new faces (strangers)** --- people you have never seen before

- **sister-in-law** --- your brother/sister's wife, your husband/wife's sister

- **get-go** --- the start

- **hit it off** --- to have a friendly conversation with a stranger

- **establish (relationship)** --- to start a relationship with someone

- **rapport** --- a very friendly relationship

- **journalist** --- a person who writes news stories as their job

- **trade (business)** --- a type of business

- **produce (film/music)** --- to manage a show, movie, or recording

- **media** --- internet, newspapers, games, TV, books, movies, music ...

- **greet** --- to say hello or welcome someone

- **nieces** --- your sisters' or brothers' daughters

- **nephews** --- your sisters' or brothers' sons

- **backyard** --- the place behind a house

- **include** --- to make something a part of something else

- **task [noun]** ---a piece of work to do

- **leave (responsibility)** --- to trust someone to do something

- **photographer** --- a person who takes photos as their job or hobby

- **grow late** --- *(formal)* to get late

- **voice (opinion)** --- to say what you really think about something

- **concerns (worries)** --- worries

• **burn out (work)** --- to work so hard that you cannot work anymore

• **consider (think)** --- to think carefully about something

• **advise (suggest)** --- to give someone advice

Comprehension Questions

1. What was John's uncle's profession?
    A) Electrical engineer
    B) Civil engineer
    C) Chemical engineer
    D) Mechanical engineer

2. Michael and Joanne's parents were John's...
    A) grandfather and grandmother.
    B) mother and father.
    C) aunt and uncle.
    D) brother and sister.

3. John's sister-in-law was married to whom?
    A) His brother
    B) His father
    C) His cousin
    D) His boss

4. Where were the kids playing during the family gathering?
    A) At the school
    B) In the house
    C) In the backyard
    D) In the toy room

5. When you are highly qualified to do a job you are called...

    A) an amateur.

    B) the workforce.

    C) an occupation.

    D) a professional.

CHAPTER TEN:

EDUCATION

With a full-time job and a girlfriend, John's **schedule** was pretty **tightly packed**. But for the sake of a better future, he **enrolled** in a **graduate program** for **economics** at his local university. John had already completed an **undergraduate** program and **graduated** with a **bachelor's degree** in **philosophy**, yet like most **liberal arts** degrees, it was not the greatest choice for **seeking employment** and starting a **career**.

This time would be different. With much more **experience** and **wisdom**, this opportunity to **further** his education would not **go wasted**. A graduate program in economics was going to be a **formidable challenge**, but if he **succeeded**, the **rewards** would be great. The classes he took at **community college** would be a **cakewalk compared** to this. Intense study and **perseverance** would be required.

The **textbooks** would often prove to be much more useful than the **lectures**. Some of the professors he had talked with such **long-winded delivery** that it was **incredibly** difficult to maintain **focus** in class. He could spend half the time reading chapters from the book and **come away with** double the information he got in the lecture **hall**. The teaching **assistants**, however, were most helpful, as they could explain **complex concepts** using very **basic** language.

To make the information **stick**, serious work was needed to be done outside the classroom. Study groups **organized** by students were **instrumental** in **providing** John the **motivation** and **drive** required to do well in the course. In the groups, students shared the **notes** they took in class and **reviewed** the information they thought would **appear** on the exams. Not all this time was serious though, as there were **multiple** breaks where **chit-chat** was **encouraged** as a **means** to **vent built-up** stress and **frustration**.

Finals for the first year were **approaching**, and anxiety filled the classroom during the last few lectures. On the test would be **essay questions** only; there would be no **multiple choice**. **Cramming wasn't** going to **get** you **anywhere** on this test. You had to know the information **in order to** get a good **grade**. John and all his classmates paid **hefty tuition fees**, but not all would pass the test. It would be those who **attended** the lectures, **participated** in the study groups, and read **extensively** that would pass with high **marks**.

It was very much like learning a **foreign** language. Those who do the best are those who **immerse** themselves in the foreign language. They read as much as possible in the **target language**, and when they can **no longer** read, they spend all their free time listening to the target language. Immersion **takes precedence** over their old hobbies and **lifestyles**. That's how they **achieve** high levels of **fluency**.

The question is not whether or not John passed the final exam. The true question is whether or not you will do **what it takes** in order to achieve fluency.

Happy studying! And thank you for reading!

Vocabulary

- **education** --- teaching and learning

- **schedule [noun]** --- a plan of things with times they will happen

- **tightly** --- closely

- **packed** --- completely full

- **enroll** --- to join or make someone join a course or college

- **graduate program** --- a course for people with a college degree

- **economics** --- the study of how money is made and used

- **undergraduate** --- a college student who does not have a degree

- **graduate (finish)** --- to complete school or college

- **bachelor's degree** --- the first degree you get from college

- **philosophy (subject)** --- the study of what human life means

- **liberal arts** --- college subjects like history, language, and art

- **seek** --- to look for

- **employment** --- having a paid job

- **career** --- a job or group of jobs you do for one type of work

- **experience (learning)** --- learning from doing things

- **wisdom** --- the power to make smart decisions

- **further [verb]** --- to grow

- **go + adjective** --- to become worse in some way

- **wasted (not used)** --- wasn't used and now can't be used

- **formidable** --- powerful or difficult

- **challenge (difficulty)** --- something that is difficult

- **succeed (achieve)** --- to complete what you planned to do

- **rewards** --- good things given after doing good things

- **community college** --- *(in the US)* a two-year local college

- **cakewalk** --- something that is very easy to do

- **compare** --- to think about how two or more things are the same and different

- **perseverance** --- continuing to try even though it's hard

- **textbooks [noun]** --- books used in school to teach a subject

- **lectures (education)** --- talks to teach a subject to a group of people

- **long-winded** --- uses too many words

- **delivery (speaking)** --- the way someone talks

- **incredibly (extremely)** --- very

- **focus [noun]** --- the center of attention

- **come away with** --- to leave a place with a feeling

- **hall (large place)** --- a large room or building for events

- **assistants [noun]** --- people who help other people

- **complex [adjective]** --- hard to understand

- **concepts** --- ideas

- **basic** --- easy to understand

- **stick (in your mind)** --- to remember clearly for a long time

- **organize (plan)** --- to do things to make plans happen

- **instrumental (necessary)** --- important

- **provide (offer)** --- to give

- **motivation (desire)** --- the feeling of wanting to do something

- **drive** --- a strong feeling of wanting to do something

- **notes (records)** --- information written by hand

- **review (study)** --- to look again at something you studied before

- **appear (be seen)** --- to start to be seen

- **multiple** --- many

- **chit-chat** --- conversation that isn't important

- **encourage (inspire)** --- to make someone feel like doing sth.

- **means** --- a way of doing something

- **vent [verb]** --- to show your negative feelings by talking

- **built-up** --- made bigger by adding many parts

- **frustration** --- an angry feeling you get because you can't do sth.

- **finals** --- exams taken at the end of college courses

- **approach (get near)** --- to come closer to something

- **essay questions** --- test questions you answer with lots of writing

- **multiple choice** --- a question with a list of possible answers to choose from

- **cramming (study)** --- studying a lot in very little time before a test

- **not get anywhere** --- to not improve at something

- **in order to** --- to be able to

- **grade (score)** --- a letter or number to show how good sth. is

- **hefty** --- large

- **tuition fees** --- money students pay colleges for teaching

- **attend (go to)** --- to go to something

- **participate** --- to join

- **extensively** --- in a large way

- **marks (scores)** --- letters or numbers to show how good sth. is

- **foreign (country)** --- from a different country

- **immerse (be involved)** --- to do nothing but one thing only

- **target language** --- the language you are trying to learn

- **no longer** --- not anymore

- **take precedence** --- to be more important than something else

- **lifestyle** --- a way of living

- **achieve** --- to complete what you planned to do

- **fluency (language)** --- able to speak a language easily and well

- **what it takes** --- the things needed to do something

Comprehension Questions

1. Where was John taking economic classes?
    A) Through an online program
    B) At a local university
    C) At a community college
    D) Through a tutor

2. When we say a challenge is formidable, we mean it is...
    A) easy.
    B) impossible.
    C) intimidating.
    D) possible.

3. What was the problem with the lectures?
    A) The classes took place late at night.
    B) John's friends were talking during class.
    C) The professor's explanations were too complicated.
    D) The professor didn't like the students.

4. Who organized the study groups?
    A) The students
    B) The teacher assistants
    C) John
    D) The professor

5. The final exam was what kind of test?
    A) All multiple choice
    B) A mix between multiple choice and essay questions
    C) A mix between cramming and hefty tuition fees
    D) Essay questions only

ABOUT THE AUTHOR

Language Guru is a brand created by a hardcore language enthusiast with a passion for creating simple but great products. They work with a large team of native speakers from across the world to make sure each product is the absolute best quality it can be.

Each product and new edition represents the opportunity to surpass themselves and previous works. The key to achieving this has always been to work from the perspective of the learner.

DID YOU ENJOY THE READ?

Thank you so much for taking the time to read our book! We hope you have enjoyed it and learned tons of vocabulary in the process.

If you would like to support our work, please consider writing a customer review on Amazon, Goodreads, or wherever you purchased our book. It would mean the world to us!

We read each and every single review posted, and we use all the feedback we receive to write even better books.

ANSWER KEY

Chapter 1:
1) D
2) B
3) B
4) B
5) A

Chapter 2:
1) C
2) D
3) B
4) C
5) C

Chapter 3:
1) B
2) C
3) A
4) D
5) B

Chapter 4:
1) D
2) B
3) A
4) C
5) C

Chapter 5:
1) D
2) C
3) A
4) D
5) B

Chapter 6:
1) D
2) B
3) B
4) A
5) C

Chapter 7:
1) D
2) C
3) A
4) C
5) B

Chapter 8:
1) B
2) A
3) C
4) B
5) A

Chapter 9:
1) D
2) C
3) A
4) C
5) D

Chapter 10:
1) B
2) C
3) C
4) A
5) D

Lightning Source UK Ltd.
Milton Keynes UK
UKHW010125200422
401743UK00001B/114

9 781950 321285